CUTTING EDGE
TECHNOLOGY

Cutting Edge Entertainment Technology

Stuart A. Kallen

ReferencePoint Press®

San Diego, CA

About the Author

Stuart A. Kallen is the author of more than 350 nonfiction books for children and young adults. He has written on topics ranging from the theory of relativity to the art of electronic dance music. In addition, Kallen has written award-winning children's videos and television scripts. In his spare time he is a singer, songwriter, and guitarist in San Diego.

© 2017 ReferencePoint Press, Inc.
Printed in the United States

For more information, contact:
ReferencePoint Press, Inc.
PO Box 27779
San Diego, CA 92198
www.ReferencePointPress.com

LIBRARY OF CONGRESS CATALOGING-IN-PUBLICATION DATA

Names: Kallen, Stuart A., 1955- author.
Title: Cutting edge entertainment technology / by Stuart A. Kallen.
Description: San Diego, CA : ReferencePoint Press, Inc., [2017] | Series:
    Cutting edge technology | Audience: Age 9-12. | Includes bibliographical
    references and index.
Identifiers: LCCN 2016004752 (print) | LCCN 2016017154 (ebook) | ISBN
    9781682820407 (hardback) | ISBN 9781682820414 (eBook)
Subjects: LCSH: Amusements--Technological innovations--Juvenile literature.
Classification: LCC GV1203 .K326 2017 (print) | LCC GV1203 (ebook) | DDC
    790--dc23
LC record available at https://lccn.loc.gov/2016004752

Contents

Innovations in Entertainment Technology

1922
The first 3D movie, *Power of Love*, previews in Los Angeles.

1998
The first portable MP3 music player, MPMan, is sold to the public.

1996
The first high-definition television broadcast occurs in Raleigh, North Carolina.

1994
Sony releases the original PlayStation video game console.

1920	1940	1960	1980	2000

1984
The first 4D movie, *The Sensorium*, premieres at the Six Flags theme park in Baltimore, Maryland, with viewers experiencing shaking seats and a series of smells released in sync with the film.

1995
Nintendo introduces Virtual Boy, a tabletop virtual reality headset that only displays red images on a black background.

1987
Computer scientist Jaron Lanier popularizes the term *virtual reality* to describe the experience of using the goggles and gloves developed by his company, VPL Research.

2006
The first GoPro Digital HERO wearable cameras are sold.

2014
Facebook founder Mark Zuckerberg buys Oculus VR for $2 billion, a move that helps generate widespread public interest in virtual reality.

2013
The first Google Glass headsets, or optical head-mounted displays, are sold to qualified testers.

2015
The annual New York City Drone Film Festival is launched to bring attention to cutting edge movies shot with wearable cameras mounted on drones.

2009
Best-selling open-world video game *Minecraft* is released.

| 2005 | 2008 | 2011 | 2014 | 2017 |

2007
The Red Digital Cinema Camera Company introduces the world's first digital movie camera that captures 4K ultra-high-definition images.

2016
Virtual reality headsets are sold to the public for the first time.

2005
Researchers at the University of Texas create the first holographic display that produces freestanding 3D video images.

Immersed in Entertainment

Human beings perceive the world through five senses: sight, smell, hearing, taste, and touch. Listening to recorded music generally involves one sense—hearing. Watching television programs or movies involves a combination of sight and sound. But researchers are working to add other senses to the entertainment experience.

In the not-too-distant future, people will expect to see, hear, and feel their entertainment. They might even be able to experience tastes and smells associated with a film, video game, or theme park attraction. As all five senses engage, people will feel completely surrounded by—or immersed in—the entertainment experience.

Virtual Reality

Immersion entertainment is already allowing users to feel as if they are physically present in a nonphysical, electronic environment. The experience is being provided by an array of high-tech virtual reality (VR) devices. Users experience an enhanced sense of sight by viewing ultra-high-definition (Ultra HD) curved screens and 3D displays. Incredibly clear, crisp sounds are provided by high-definition (HD) speakers and headsets.

Developers are working to add the dimension of touch to the 3D world of immersion entertainment. The sense of touch can be stimulated by electronic sensors that physically convey to the user feelings of motion and changes in temperature. The tactile sensors attach to the head, hands, feet, and other body parts and can be put on before a user sits down to watch a TV show or play a video game.

The immersive experience is also coming to movie theaters. Seats are being developed that contain built-in sensors in the seat, back, and armrests. The 4D seats will shake, tilt, twist, heat, and cool with the action as it unfolds on the screen.

In coming years people will be able to visit entire entertainment environments that will make them feel like they are inside a movie. Interactive rooms will project images, sounds, feelings, and smells. These rooms might be located at theme parks, where users will interact with the entertainment through touch, voice commands, and hand and body gestures.

immersion

The act of being involved deeply in an activity or experience.

Immersion entertainment allows users to feel as if they are physically present in a non-physical, electronic environment. The experience uses a variety of high-tech virtual reality (VR) devices like the headset pictured here.

Some Nerves and Brainwaves

Some scientists are already looking beyond virtual reality. They want to connect the entertainment experience directly to a user's central nervous system through a series of sensors worn on the head, spine, and other body parts. This futuristic system could provide total immersion into virtual reality by artificially stimulating the nerves and brainwaves.

tactile

Connected with the sense of touch or designed to be perceived by touch.

Total immersion users might simply sit in a chair hooked up to wires with all five senses engaged in an entertainment experience. With this technology a user might battle aliens in a distant galaxy, romp with cartoon characters in an animated environment, enjoy a gourmet meal in nineteenth-century France, or climb Mount Everest.

New Worlds

While scientists work to perfect virtual reality, there are some who are anxious about the technology. Research shows that video games can be addictive. Binge players suffer from a number of physical and mental symptoms, including depression, headaches, and stress. There are fears that total immersion virtual reality entertainment might be even more habit-forming than traditional video games. Some imagine a future resembling a science fiction movie in which millions live in a virtual vacuum while blocking out the world around them.

Such concerns are not dampening enthusiasm for virtual reality—one of the hottest trends in 2016. Major tech and electronics companies, including Facebook, Google, Samsung, and HTC, were racing to market VR devices. These corporations hope to make VR headsets and handsets as ubiquitous as smartphones. And this is seen as only the beginning. As researchers work to put experiences directly inside people's heads, new worlds will open up. All the senses will be totally immersed in experiences limited only by the human imagination.

CHAPTER ONE

Music and Concerts

Hearing is the sense most often associated with music, but songs engage other senses as well. Music is made of sound waves, physical vibrations that the ears transform into electrical signals interpreted as music by the brain. And as anyone who has been to a live concert knows, sound waves from loud music can shake the entire body. This makes music tactile, or perceived by the sense of touch. Watching musicians make music also engages the sensory element of sight.

When the sounds, vibrations, and visuals of music are mixed in the brain, emotions and memories are triggered. For this reason, sad or beautiful songs can make a listener cry. A happy or energetic song can elicit whoops of joy and make listeners get up and dance.

As a physical and emotional experience, music is one of the oldest forms of entertainment. Some scientists believe that when humans evolved 2 million years ago, they played music even before they learned to communicate with speech. Today researchers are trying to take the science of music to a new level as they search for new and exciting ways to enhance the musical experience.

Measuring, Math, and Music

Music begins with musical instruments, and musicians and engineers are constantly looking for new ways to produce unique sounds. Some are developing software applications based on what is called sonification. The sonification process uses numerical data to create sound and music.

To sonify something is to take any type of measurement and turn it into sound. A heart rate monitor used in a hospital provides a good example; the beeping sound the monitor makes is a sonification of the rhythm of a patient's heartbeat. When the heart beats fast, the monitor beeps rapidly, and when the heart slows, so does the beeping. When the heart stops, the monitor emits an unbroken tone some might interpret as somber.

Beyond heartbeats, music can be made from almost any type of numerical measurement, including those taken from charts, graphs, and formulas. Music has been made based on the numerical patterns of traffic on a busy highway, the ups and downs of the stock market, and complex formulas devised by physicists. The sounds of sonification are most often produced on a synthesizer, an electronic musical instrument that can imitate traditional instruments or generate unique tones.

sonification

The process of converting mathematical data into sounds or music.

New Ways of Making Music

The most unusual modern methods of mixing math and music have roots in ancient Greece. Around 500 BCE the Greek philosopher Pythagoras wrote that all science and art could be reduced to mathematical equations. Pythagoras understood that the sound of a musical note on a stringed instrument could be measured mathematically; a string that was longer in length made a lower note than a string that was of shorter length. Pythagoras did not know that sound was vibration, but when higher notes are plucked a string vibrates faster, and when low notes are played a string vibrates slower. These measurable vibrations are called frequencies.

Pythagoras applied his understanding of string lengths to the movements of planets in a theory he called the harmony of the spheres. The theory was based on the various speeds that the moon, planets, and stars move across the sky. Comparing planets to strings, Pythagoras theorized that the movements create musical harmony in the universe that cannot be perceived by humans. Not everyone agreed with Pythagoras's harmony of the spheres concept; philosophers, astronomers, and scholars debated the theory for centuries.

In the early twenty-first century, scientists determined that harmonies might actually emanate from the planets, stars, and other

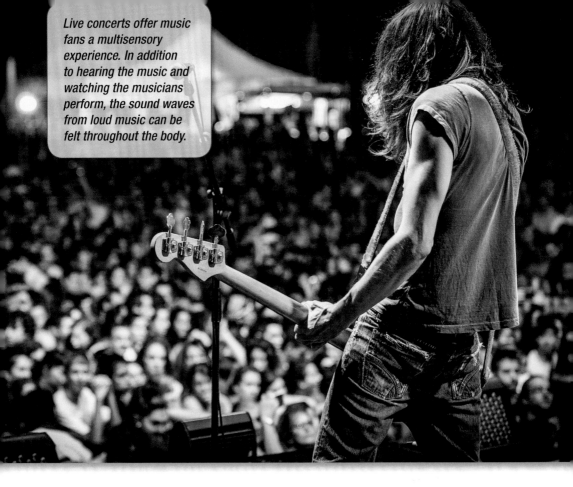

celestial bodies for reasons never understood by Pythagoras. It is now known that objects in space emit electromagnetic radiation that creates frequencies outside the range of human hearing. Although the objects may not be musical, the sounds they emit can be scaled to human hearing—and used to create music that has never been heard before.

Lucianne Walkowicz is a musician and astrophysicist who is part of the Kepler space observatory mission run by NASA. The Kepler is a space telescope used to search for earthlike planets orbiting distant stars. The search for alien worlds inspired Walkowicz to compose music based on star-generated frequencies that were measured by the Kepler. As Walkowicz explains: "I take the data and search for which frequencies are present at different times, then scale them to frequencies the human ear can hear. Then I create tones that change with time to represent how the frequencies in the star are changing. As you listen, the sounds change as the frequencies change."[1] Walkowicz believes the resulting sounds provide a unique musical history of each star. These sounds have never been made before and can be used by scientists to identify individual stars.

Computer artwork depicts the Kepler space telescope. Musician and astrophysicist Lucianne Walkowicz uses star-generated frequencies, which are measured by the Kepler, to compose music.

While the star music is helpful to scientists, Walkowicz adds an artistic element by mixing in sounds from Earth. On the 2013 song "Powerful Protector," the music of the stars is blended with Buddhist chants. Walkowicz explains the reason she melds art, science, and religion: "I chose these chants for their rhythmic qualities, similar in nature to the . . . frequencies of the stars I study."[2]

Sonifying Objects

German art professor Dennis P. Paul was interested in sonification and decided to build a machine that creates sounds from any object. Paul calls it "an instrument for the sonification of everyday things."[3] The instrument consists of an aluminum stand, which holds a clamp that turns like a barbeque spit. Household objects like a shoe, shampoo bottle, or crumpled newspaper can be placed in the clamp. The clamp is slowly rotated by a small motor. As an object turns, its shape is measured by a high-precision laser.

Paul created custom-made software to turn the variations of the object's surface into audio frequencies, notes, and musical scales. The motor that rotates the object can be sped up or slowed down to change the sounds. As Paul explains: "A variety of everyday objects can be mounted into the instrument. Their silhouettes define loops, melodies and rhythms. Thus mundane things are reinterpreted as musical notation. Playing the instrument is a mixture of practice, anticipation, and serendipity [luck]."[4]

Like the starlight music made by Walkowicz, Paul's sonification of objects lacks traditional musical qualities. However, both are unique forms of music that could not be made without cutting edge technology.

New Ways of Listening

Walkowicz's music of the stars can be streamed from the Internet or downloaded to a digital music player. Although countless people stream music or listen to digital files every day, rock musician Neil Young is not happy about the quality of the music. Young rose to fame in the 1960s as a singer-songwriter who played in bands including Buffalo Springfield and Crosby, Stills, Nash & Young. Since the early 2010s Young has been one of the most prominent critics of the way digital music is produced and sold.

Most online music files are sold in two formats: MP3 or the AAC format used by Apple. Both digital sound formats were developed in the 1990s to shrink the size of the files used on CDs. This made digital music easier to download from the Internet and store on a computer or other device. The problem some critics see with MP3 and AAC files is that they are compressed. This means bits of data—sounds listeners will supposedly not miss—are permanently removed. The more data that is removed, the smaller the file. However, when sound data is removed, the music is of lower quality.

Young says songs in the MP3 and AAC formats sound terrible when compared to high-resolution, or hi-res, digital music formats such as FLAC (Free Lossless Audio Codec). A FLAC file has 90 percent more digital information than an MP3 file. Put another way, MP3s contain only 10 percent of the digital sound information of a FLAC file. And when most musicians record in a studio, they create even higher quality digital files known as Waveform, or WAV. WAVs have twice as much sound information as FLAC files. With MP3s, Young says, consumers cannot hear the music that musicians intended them to hear: "I have a little bit of trouble with the quality of the sound of music today. I don't like it. It just makes me angry. . . . MP3s feature only 5% of the data from an original master file. . . . If you're an artist and you created something and you knew the master was 100% great, but the consumer got 5%, would you be feeling good?"[5]

Young was so angry that he created a crowd-funding campaign on Kickstarter in 2014. The money was to be used to create a new digital music player called Pono and a music service called PonoMusic. (*Pono* means "righteous" in Hawaiian.) Young's idea to create a cutting edge high-quality music player was popular; the Kickstarter campaign met its goal of $800,000 in ten hours. By the time the campaign was over, 18,220 people backed the campaign, pledging $6,225,354.

The Space Composer

Robert Alexander has an impressive job title. He is the sonification specialist for the Solar and Heliospheric Research Group (SHRG) at the University of Michigan. The SHRG works with the space agency NASA to study the sun, but Alexander is not a scientist. He is a classically trained composer who combines sounds and science to make music from the sun.

When Alexander began working as a sonification specialist with SHRG, he was shown dramatic movies taken of the surface of the sun. Sudden flashes of brightness called solar flares could be seen shooting thousands of miles into space. The solar flares contained more energy than thousands of atomic bombs, but there was no soundtrack; the movies were silent. However, Alexander understood that the rise and fall of solar activity could be translated into patterns on graphs. He matched drums to some of the rhythms on the graphs, and other data patterns were used to generate melodies played by cellos, violins, and synthesizers. Through Alexander's work, scientists learned they could hear trends associated with solar flares better than they could observe them with their eyes. This led NASA to hire Alexander to continue his work with sonification.

Pono is designed to play FLAC and WAV files. Young explained the virtues of his hi-res music player: "Everyone who's ever heard Pono will tell you that the difference is surprising and dramatic. They tell us that not only do they hear the difference; they feel it in their body, in their soul."[6]

The Pono player became available for purchase in early 2015. The $400 device plays songs of FLAC quality or higher. However, hi-res albums cost about twice as much as MP3 downloads from other sources. Pono was endorsed by best-selling musicians, including Norah Jones, Jack White, Tom Petty, Arcade Fire, and others. However, tests run by numerous music critics found that most people cannot hear the difference between hi-res Pono music and typical MP3 files that can be played on smartphones. As critic Seth Stevenson of *Slate* explained: "I listened as intensely as I could, to appreciate every subtle nuance. I opened my mind to the music, praying for sonic distinctions to emerge. But if there was any difference between the Pono and the iPhone, I simply couldn't detect it."[7]

Whatever the critics might say, the demand for hi-res sound is growing. Audiophiles—people obsessed with high-quality music reproduction—can buy a high-resolution Walkman for around $1,200 or an Astell & Kern AK240 music player for $2,500. And there are numerous other hi-res music players on the market meant to change the way people listen to music.

High-Resolution Speakers

When hi-res music is played through high-quality audio systems, the results can be awe-inspiring; hi-res loudspeakers can provide musical details that are nearly equal to a live performance. Such speaker systems can cost $150,000 or more. But designers in Stockholm, Sweden, are providing a cutting edge hi-res experience unlike any other for much less money. A speaker system called the AudioOrb, created by Studio Total and the experimental designer Petter Johansson, can be purchased for $15,000.

The AudioOrb is a sound environment that listeners can climb into. It consists of a clear plastic sphere about 6 feet (1.8 m) in diameter. The sphere is packed with eighteen high-fidelity speakers that produce a full, rich spectrum of sound. Listeners sitting inside the globe cannot hear any outside noises that might interfere with their ultimate audiophile experience. The speakers are surrounded by pillows so listeners can recline in comfort.

Studio Total produces other cutting edge hi-res speakers. The company's Wall of Sound system contains twenty-eight ground-shaking speakers in a flat-panel 3-by-4-foot (91 by 122 cm) cabinet. The Wall of Sound is made to be hooked into an MP3 player. The company calls it the world's most powerful iPod dock.

Community Connections

The AudioOrb isolates listeners who want to hear every subtle note and beat in their music. But the fastest-growing trend in musical entertainment—electronic dance music (EDM)—is based on providing sensory overload for its fans. EDM is known for its pumping bass, flashing lights, and wild dancing.

Those who attend huge annual EDM festivals like the Electric Daisy Carnival in Las Vegas, Nevada, and TomorrowWorld in Chattahoochee Hills, Georgia, do more than see, hear, and feel the music. They also share a sense of community through dancing and a collective love of the music. Journalist Sierra Vandervort describes her experience at EDM concerts: "Everyone's your best friend. . . . No hand goes without a high-five, no introduction goes without a hug and you never have to dance alone. . . . There's a sense of community at EDM shows you can't find anywhere else. It's communication without words."[8]

SFX Entertainment, which produces TomorrowWorld and the associated Tomorrowland fest in Belgium, understands the community connection of EDM. And the company is using the latest technology to enhance that experience in ways that have never been tried before. The three-day TomorrowWorld festival attracts about 160,000, but the large group is linked together by electronic wristbands provided to all who attend. The wristbands, which cost SFX about ten dollars each to produce, have been used since 2014 to replace traditional paper tickets. They are mailed to concertgoers weeks before the event, and users activate their wristbands online. On the day of the concert, the wristbands are scanned at the gate to allow wearers access to festival grounds.

Aside from eliminating the problem of lost tickets, the TomorrowWorld wristbands encourage friendship. When two users press the heart button on the wristbands at the same time, they link to one another's Facebook page so they can continue their festival friendship after the show. As EDM reviewer Peter Rubinstein explains, this feature is "an impressive and innovative first step towards making the festival community even more inclusive."[9]

The TomorrowWorld wristband is also part of the entertainment experience. The bracelets have two embedded light-emitting diodes (LEDs) that are remotely controlled by the crew that operates the stage lights. When activated, the wristbands sync with colors that match the light show onstage. As tech reviewer Jelmer Tiete writes, "This is a pretty neat effect, especially when a couple thousand people are waving their hands in the air."[10]

Full Party Immersion

Tech at Tomorrowland and TomorrowWorld is being used to bring the festival experience to those who cannot attend the event or want to relive their memories. Official videos such as *Tomorrowland 2014: 360 Degrees of Madness* feature a navigation button that allows users to travel through the event and see the action from every angle.

The videos were shot by a virtual tour company, YouVisit, to create what it calls "360 degree full party immersion."[11] The

Concert-goers at the Tomorrowland Festival in Belgium display their electronic wristbands. In addition to replacing traditional paper tickets, the wristbands are embedded with LED lights that can sync with colors to match the light show on stage.

Transporting Listeners

With hi-res speakers, each instrument on a recording is crisply defined and distinct from other instruments in the musical mix. Bass notes are not only heard with the ears but are felt vibrating in the breastbone. Audiophile Fred Kaplan describes the experience of listening to hi-res speakers: "The musicians seemed to be playing and singing in the room with me, their voices and instruments so vivid, almost 3-D, imbued with the tonal colors and emotional heft of the real thing. . . . [The listener is] transported to the place where the players laid this music down, hearing it the way the mics . . . and mixing boards took it down."

Fred Kaplan, "I, Audiophile," *Slate*, February 20, 2015. www.slate.com.

experience is provided by YouVisit camera operators, who wear custom camera rigs with multiple cameras that capture high-definition 360-degree photos and videos of the event. The result is a virtual festival experience that allows watchers to explore the entire festival on an Internet browser or smartphone. Those who own virtual reality goggles can enjoy the experience as if they were in attendance.

The 360-degree full party immersion experience takes viewers from the campgrounds to the heart of the dance floor. Viewers can see sunsets or experience the concert from the perspective of a headlining DJ. As Rubinstein writes:

> With these 360-degree pictures and 360-degree films you can again experience and feel the depth and breadth of the moments we yearn to hold on to forever, but our human memories only allow to fade. No longer will that be a problem for The People of Tomorrow with . . . advancements in experience technology. Forever we shall remember exactly what it was like to look around us and take in the sights.[12]

Weather-Related Glitches

TomorrowWorld may be at the leading edge of EDM festival technology, but the 2015 event also showed that technology cannot fix typical concert problems. There was continuous rain throughout the three-day festival, and the 8,000-acre (3,237 ha) concert site turned into a huge mud pit. Shuttle services designed to efficiently whisk people to and from the venue were hampered by the storms. This left thousands of people in distant parking lots with little access to water, food, or restrooms.

sensory

Relating to sensation or the physical senses; sent by or perceived by the senses.

The numerous weather-related problems forced SFX to close the festival on the last day to those not already camping on the grounds. This created anger among the single-day attendees who had valid wristbands for the last day but were denied access. Hundreds attempted to crash the gates. For those inside the festival, the smell of wet bodies and the taste of mud was probably not the type of sensory overload they hoped to achieve at the high-tech festival.

CHAPTER TWO

Television Trends

In 2015 the average American spent nearly five hours a day watching television. And that figure does not include the hours people spent streaming content on computers, tablets, and smartphones. But in recent years streaming services like Netflix, Amazon Prime, Hulu, and others have changed the way people watch television.

Streaming services provide instant access to TV shows and movies. The services also produce their own award-winning series such as *House of Cards* and *Transparent*. This new television content, offered in new ways, is luring people away from ad-based programming provided by traditional networks and cable TV channels. As a result, the number of people "pulling the plug" on their cable service is expected to rise about 3 percent a year for the foreseeable future.

TV on the Internet

Viewers are embracing the freedom of watching TV whenever, wherever, and however they want. This has led to steady growth in the number of people watching TV on the Internet. Researchers working for the video streaming software company Adobe Systems confirmed the trend by tracking more than 1.5 billion log-ins to online sites like Netflix and Amazon Prime Video in 2013 and 2014. The study showed a new trend: The number of people viewing TV on the Internet grew by nearly four times—388 percent—in a single year. As tech business writer Marcus Wohlsen explains: "The Internet is where people want to watch. In more and more homes, online TV isn't a geeky novelty, a sidelight to the traditional version. It's just what TV looks like now."[13]

The growth is due to new apps, new sites for watching, and more content available online. And unlike traditional TV, online shows do not require viewers to commit to a single piece of hardware. From 2013 to 2014, the number of people streaming

TV with gaming consoles and digital media streamers like Roku and Apple TV tripled. And though it may seem ironic during an era when televisions are getting bigger and better, more people are watching TV on their smartphones. Around half of all online TV in 2014 was streamed with iPhone apps.

Eyeball TV

Another trendsetting piece of TV-watching hardware is categorized as mediawear. In 2015 the tech company Avegant introduced the Glyph headset, mediawear made for seeing and hearing TV shows in a completely new way. The Glyph looks like a pair of large headphones with a plastic band that flips down in front of the wearer's eyes. The Glyph's flip-down band contains a set of lenses and tiny mirrors that reflect light directly onto the user's retinas, the part of the eye responsible for sight. The device maker calls this Retinal Imaging Technology. This technology mimics the way people perceive light in an every-day environment. The Glyph can be used to watch 2D and 3D videos, play video games, and listen to music. Tech reviewer David Pierce describes the experience: "Whatever you watch in the Glyph takes up the same amount of your view that a 65-inch TV in your living room does, or the huge screen in a theater. But you can look down and see your hands, or up and see the sky. . . . It's a personal movie theater, the head-phones and screen giving you a private and high-end experience."[14]

retina

A light-sensitive layer of tissue at the back of the eyeball that is responsible for creating the sense of sight.

Pierce explains that although the Glyph looks something like a virtual re-ality headset, it is not the same thing. Glyph lets users see above and below the visual field, allowing them to stay oriented to their surroundings. This is different from VR headsets, which take up a viewer's complete field of vision and provide a 360-degree display. When users turn their heads, they see a different display, making it seem as if they are in an alternate reality. The VR experience can cause eyestrain or dizzi-ness, neither of which is a problem with the Glyph.

TV on the Wall

Dave Evans does not believe that a headset—even a high-tech one like the Glyph—represents the future of TV. Evans is chief fu-turist at Cisco Systems; the company pays him to predict events as they will unfold in the coming years. When Evans looks at the future of TV, he envisions that future on a wall. And he does not mean a wall-mounted flat-screen TV. As Evans writes: "I mean that your whole wall could literally be a television screen, giving you a window on the world in any way you want it to. [By 2024] streamed video [will appear] on every square inch of wall in a mid-size home."[15]

TV on the wall will rely on two developments: more bandwidth and ultra-thin, flexible video displays. Bandwidth is the speed at which digital information flows from the Internet to a device. Bandwidth is typically delivered to homes through broadband cable connections and to mobile devices by 3G or 4G network connections.

In 2015 nearly 70 percent of Americans had broadband cable at home. Although this was adequate bandwidth for streaming TV, it would not be enough to stream wall-sized content. However, in 2013 Google rolled out a new network called Google Fiber in Kansas City, Kansas. The network was expanded to Austin, Texas; Atlanta, Georgia; Nashville, Tennessee; and elsewhere in subsequent years. Fiber delivers Internet speeds that are about one hundred times faster than the average broadband connection in the United States. This speed would allow video to appear all across the wall.

Once bandwidth is available, wall TV would need other cutting edge concepts to function, as Evans explains: "There are people right now experimenting with ultra thin flexible displays and smart

In an era when televisions are getting bigger and better, more people are choosing to watch TV on their smartphones. Between 2013 and 2014, the number of people viewing TV on the Internet nearly quadrupled.

coatings spread on the wall like cream cheese that will enable you to turn any room of your house into a communications and entertainment portal."[16]

Thin as Wallpaper

Although coatings that produce television images do not yet exist, ultra-thin displays are already being developed by the South Korean electronics company LG. In 2015 LG unveiled an ultra-thin, flexible concept television that was 55 inches (140 cm) across but only about $\frac{3}{64}$ of an inch (1 mm) thick—about the same thickness as a DVD. (The thickness of a typical television is about 3 inches, or 76 mm.) LG's TV, which weighed about 4 pounds (1.8 kg), sticks to the wall using a thin magnetic base. The entire TV could be peeled off the wall and moved to a magnet base mounted on a wall in a different location. The flexible TV could also be rolled up and stored in a plastic tube when not in use.

The LG television is based on organic light-emitting diode (OLED) technology. In the twenty-first century, LEDs have become commonplace for use in home lighting, car headlights, and traffic signals. LEDs are also used in screens found on smartphones, televisions, and computer monitors. But OLEDs are much thinner and can be used to produce displays not much thicker than wallpaper. OLEDs use less energy than LEDs and produce pictures of much higher quality. However, OLEDs are much more expensive to produce. LG's ultra-thin TV is expected to sell for more than $12,000.

> **diode**
>
> A semiconductor device with two terminals, typically allowing the flow of current in one direction only.

The production technology for OLEDs is not yet advanced enough to produce TVs as large as a living room or bedroom wall. However, LG has plans to one day produce a 99-inch (2.5 m) OLED TV. According to scientist Ching W. Tang, the inventor of OLEDs, the large, flexible displays will be ubiquitous by 2025.

Holographic TV

Some scientists are looking beyond living room walls when researching next-generation televisions. New breakthroughs in holographic technology might one day allow TV shows to be projected into the middle of a room. The concept relies on holography, a photographic technique that creates holograms, or images that appear in three dimensions.

holography

A photographic technique that records the light scattered from an object and then presents it in a way that appears three-dimensional.

Holographic TVs would create free-standing 3D images that seem real. Viewers could walk through the holographic picture, look around, peek behind objects, and view lifelike images from every angle. The technology might be used to provide experiences like riding a roller coaster or taking off into outer space. With holographic technology, viewers will not have to wear special 3D glasses or virtual reality headsets to see the moving images.

Although the promise of holographic TV is exciting, many complex technical problems must be overcome to make holographic action a reality. For example, production costs would be extremely high for holographic TV. Making holographic video requires up to sixty-four HD cameras to focus on and follow the movements of each actor. The resulting images are reconstructed on computers running 3D-imaging software. The computers send the information to laser projectors designed to broadcast natural-looking images in a viewer's room.

Despite the tech issues, Massachusetts Institute of Technology (MIT) researcher Michael Bove believes holographic TV will be a reality by 2023. And the sets will cost little more than today's televisions. Bove runs MIT's Technology Media Lab, where researchers have been working to develop a holographic chip, or semiconductor, since the late 1980s. In 2013 the lab successfully created a chip called a spatial light modulator. The chip bends projected light in a range of directions, which produces a display

Life Inside a Giant Television Set

British futurist Dave Evans describes what life will be like when every wall in a home is capable of being used as a television:

How exactly will we use that [technology] enabling you to have displays on every wall and in effect live inside a giant television set? You could be cooking to follow the recipe showing on *Masterchef* which is being streamed to the tiles above your [stove]. Or you could use your walls as a portal to anywhere else in the world. You could be working with one eye on your elderly parents, through a video link to their home. Family viewing will take on a whole new meaning. On a Saturday evening you could be sitting down virtually with your whole family to watch [a TV show] together—with the program appearing on one wall, your daughter in Australia on the other, your grandchildren in America on another. Today we tend to think of video as something that is on or off, but once you can create a display on any surface, that will change. . . . Your parents or your children, wherever they are, can be with you all the time, and you will only have to walk past the particular wall that acts as your portal to them to stop and say hi.

Quoted in Zoë Clapp, ed., *2014: The Future of Television.* London: Premium, 2014, p. 20.

that simulates real-life objects. The spatial light modulator could also be used in other applications, from video games to robotic surgery. Bove says the chip costs "tens of dollars" to make and maintain: "The technology itself is one that's easy and inexpensive and, as far as we are aware . . . has never been applied to displays before."[17]

The holographic chip has already been used at MIT to successfully project holograms. One holographic video consisted of a graduate student dressed like Princess Leia in the original

An artist's depiction of a man watching 3D holographic TV is seen here. While the promise of holographic TV is exciting, many complex technical problems need to be overcome to make holographic action a reality.

Star Wars movie. The project was meant as a salute to the 1977 film, which showed Obi-Wan Kenobi watching a holograph of the princess pleading for help. Software engineer Jules Urbach compares holographic technology to another popular space show, the once futuristic cartoon *The Jetsons*, which aired in the 1960s: "Holographic video is one of those Jetson-type of things, where it's something everybody knows you have to have for you to feel like you're in the future."[18]

4D TV

While some scientists work to create realistic TV images, others are concentrating on sensory experiences that are currently left out of the viewing equation. The sense of touch can make viewers feel as if they are part of the action on the screen. The sense of smell can add to the experience. These physical elements, which provide an extra dimension to the viewing experience, are called 4D effects.

Researchers are using electronic sensors to add tactile dimensions such as rocking, rumbling, shaking, heat, and cold to TV viewing. The sensors are incorporated into gloves, belts, boots, and vests. Sensors can also work with motors and other mechanical elements to add motion to special television viewing chairs and couches. With tactile sensors, TV viewers watching a building explode or a tidal wave hit a city could experience a variety of synchronized physical effects.

A company called D-Box makes what it calls motion-enabled home theater seats that are synchronized with the on-screen action. The seats create a realistic immersive experience. D-Box marketing director Guy Marcoux provides an example: "Let's say you've got Harry Potter on his broomstick playing Quidditch. We will make you feel as if you are on that broomstick. If he banks left or right, you'll feel that, or if he drops, we create that free-floating effect. And if wind is coming, you'll feel vibration in your chair."[19]

synchronized
Occurring or operating at the same time.

The Immersive Explosion

Tactile sensors can also transmit information live from a concert or sporting event. Viewers at home who receive the information will have the feeling of "being there" that is not now available at home. Sensors attached to world-class entertainers and athletes will track the motion of their heads, hands, feet, arms, and legs, as well as their eye movements. This will allow performers to convey their personal sight, sound, and tactile experiences to millions of TV watchers. Viewers will be able to enjoy a live concert from a pop singers' point of view or a football game from the quarterback's position on the 10-yard line.

Holographic Soccer

Viewers of the 2022 FIFA World Cup soccer tournament in Japan might watch the game as a holographic television broadcast. In 2015 Japanese TV producers announced plans to capture the World Cup using two hundred HD cameras. The images will be broadcast to viewers around the world if holographic TVs are a reality by that time. If not, the games will be projected live onto empty soccer fields across the world. That means viewers will be able to go to their local stadiums and watch the soccer matches as if they were taking place right in front of their eyes, with holographic players moving around the pitch.

The popularity of tactile sensors is expected to grow, and the devices will transmit information from a wide variety of sources. As Mark Luden, CEO of the sensor company Guitammer, explained in 2015:

> We see the market for . . . tactile and motion (immersive) broadcasting exploding in the next two to five years. Literally everything and everyone—from your family pet to NFL players—will have some kind of sensor on transmitting all types of information, including location, motion and force for further use. . . . Imagine watching the next Olympics on the "Immersive Channel" . . . and being able to ski or snowboard with your favorite athlete. See what they see and feel what they feel. . . . You'll literally be in the mountains or in the half pipe.[20]

Tactile Air

Luden's vision of the future is based on production of various forms of hardware that can be installed in clothing items or chairs to provide motion. But touch technology is moving beyond the wires and gears of immersive TV. At the Walt Disney Company's Disney Research lab, scientists have developed a technology called Aireal that delivers interactive tactile experiences without users having to sit in a special chair or wear a device such as a glove with sensors. The Aireal is designed to use a vortex, or ring of air, that can travel up to 6 feet (1.8 m) while maintaining its shape and speed. When the air hits a user's skin, the low pressure system inside the vortex collapses and creates a force on the skin that simulates touch, movement, or collisions with objects.

Students at the University of Bristol in England have developed a similar device called Ultrahaptics. Instead of air, it uses ultrasonic vibrations, or sound waves, to provide feelings out of thin air.

Social Television

As TV technology evolves, it is being united with a social element. Viewers are increasingly using their smartphones or tablet computers—called second screens—to share the TV experience. In 2015 about 40 percent of adults said they looked at second screens while watching TV programs. This is motivating television show producers and actors to add live input to broadcasts using Twitter and other social media platforms. In a trend that has developed since 2013, popular shows now inspire hundreds of thousands of tweets and other online participation from viewers. But whatever the latest tech trends, people will continue to turn on the TV to be amused, thrilled, frightened, or inspired by good stories—whether they are watching on a second screen or a wall-sized wafer-thin panel.

CHAPTER THREE

Movies

In recent decades new technology has brought significant changes to moviemaking and moviegoing. Hi-definition sound systems and 3D imagery have changed how audiences perceive movies by immersing them in the on-screen action. And development of computer-generated imagery, or CGI, technology in the late 2000s has profoundly changed the visual look of films. Production of blockbusters like *Avatar* (2009), *Frozen* (2013), and *Transformers: Age of Extinction* (2014) would not have been possible without major advances in computer power and CGI software.

The Magic of Virtual Reality

The development of virtual reality represents another new chapter in filmmaking. Virtual reality headsets like the Oculus Rift and Samsung Gear VR were first made available to consumers in early 2016. Users watching films with the hands-free VR headsets are entertained by a completely immersive, computer-generated, 3D environment. The VR effect is created by lenses inside the headset that focus the picture separately for each eye. This creates a 3D "stereoscopic" image that mimics how each eye views the world from a slightly different perspective. The visuals are enhanced by a feat called head tracking. That means when the user's head moves, the picture shifts up and down, side to side, or at an angle, depending on the movements. The earpieces on a VR headset add an immersive sonic experience by providing 3D audio. This technology uses complex software to surround users with realistic sounds that seem to come from all directions.

According to tech reviewer Will Shanklin, the idea of watching a virtual reality movie is different from any other entertainment experience. Shanklin compares the feeling to magic. While wearing a Samsung Gear VR headset, he understood that he was sitting in a chair while wearing a headset, but it felt as if he were transported somewhere else: "Just enough of your brain is tricked that it feels like you've stepped into a teleporting machine. Virtual reality doesn't physically send you somewhere else, but it does give you experiences that, on a perception level, aren't too far away from that. *Magic*."[21]

Pixar Animation Studios, known for highly acclaimed animated movies such as *Toy Story*, *Cars*, *Brave*, and *Inside Out*, among others, is already moving forward with virtual reality. Pixar had at least five headset-compatible animation films in production in 2016. Entertainment reporter Steven Zeitchik says there is a "giddy enthusiasm"[22] in Hollywood about the potential of virtual reality for telling stories. Oscar-nominated documentary filmmaker Danfung Dennis explains why: "Storytelling for many centuries has been, essentially, people sitting around a campfire telling you about the buffalo hunt. . . . With virtual reality, you're on the buffalo hunt."[23]

As the technology develops, moviemakers will need to contend with a few challenges. For example, makers of horror movies might have to tone down the violence and gore for VR viewers, who will have a 360-degree, close-up view of the on-screen savagery. Additionally, VR allows users to look around an entire scene during a movie; while gazing at the sky or the floor, a viewer might miss the main action. Another problem is based on the idea that virtual reality is an isolating experience; people wearing VR headsets cannot communicate with one another. Further, it remains unclear whether viewers will want to pay money to enter a theater where they will sit with headsets strapped to their faces for two hours.

Digital Movie Cameras

While virtual reality is changing the way people tell stories, a new generation of digital movie cameras is transforming what people see on the silver screen. Ultra HD cameras are cheaper and smaller than traditional film cameras. Ultra HDs allow filmmakers to shoot crisp, vivid digital movies that can be readily manipulated using CGI software.

Ultra HD is also known as 4K, and as tech writer Nick Pino pointed out in January 2016, 4K is "the hottest techy buzzword

of the past few years, and it's a technology that's rewriting the rulebook when it comes to image quality."[24] Someone watching a movie shot in 4K can easily see the difference—the picture is incredibly sharp and engaging, and actors' skin tones are much more realistic when compared to images on film. This is due to the complex technical aspects of 4K.

The term *4K* refers to the number of pixels either captured by a camera or projected onto a screen. Pixels are tiny electronic dots of light; each pixel contains specific digital information that defines its color and brightness. A digital image consists of mil- lions of pixels, but individual pixels are too small to see without magnification. The eye naturally blends pixels together to create what appears to be a solid image. Whereas an HD image—on a typical modern TV for example—has 1,080 pixels per inch, a 4K image has around 4,000 pixels per inch. This means a 4K pic- ture has four times more definition, making it noticeably brighter, clearer, and more colorful.

The era of 4K movie cameras began in 2005. Jim Jannard, who made his fortune as the founder of the sunglasses company

Oakley, started the Red Digital Cinema Camera Company. Jannard's goal was to build the world's best cameras, which he called REDs. Jannard believed that 4K video was the future of film, and he wanted his cameras to be both high-end and affordable.

When the RED ONE was released in 2007, it was the first movie camera that was smaller, lighter, and cheaper than a film camera. Since that time, the cameras improved to capture images that might be called ultra Ultra HD; the RED EPIC (2011) could shoot 5K video, and the RED DRAGON (2013) was capable of producing eye-popping 6K films.

While producing cinema-quality images, REDs could be purchased for about $50,000, whereas a film camera cost about four times as much. By 2011 the RED was so popular that Hollywood history was made; the three companies that made traditional 35-millimeter film cameras announced they were getting out of the business. In 2015 some of Hollywood's biggest pictures were shot with RED cameras. These included *The Martian*, *Avengers: Age of Ultron*, and *X-Men Apocalypse*. And the success of RED prompted other companies, including Panasonic and Sony, to produce 4K film cameras.

While the RED transformed filmmaking for major studios, it has also made it easier for young filmmakers to produce independent films. As digital film specialist Nick Zurko wrote in 2015:

> RED was essentially ahead of its time in the company's belief that the future of film was in 4K resolution and thus sought to create a digital camera that could truly look as good, if not better than film, while being significantly smaller, more portable, and ultimately more affordable. Simply put, students who attend film school today are able to use cameras and shoot at a resolution that was just a glimmer of a possibility ten years ago.[25]

New Perspectives

Film school students have another moviemaking tool that almost no one could have imagined years earlier: small, durable, waterproof GoPro cameras that allow viewers to see the action from the filmmaker's point of view. The first GoPro digital camera, the HERO, was introduced in 2006. The wearable camera was unique; it was easy enough for a kid to use, but it took high-quality images suitable for professional filmmakers. GoPros could be worn on helmets, diving masks, headbands, wristbands, and chest harnesses. GoPros could also be mounted on vehicles, bicycles, and surfboards. By 2012 the company was selling more than 2 million cameras a year, and there were more than 10 million GoPro videos on YouTube that included surfing, skydiving, mountain biking, and other action events. Before the invention of small, wearable GoPros, these types of videos were difficult or impossible to make. Hollywood directors who were filming car chases took notice, as Go Pro founder Nicholas Woodman explains:

point of view

The position from which something or someone is observed.

> In 2009 . . . we were surprised to learn that the best selling [GoPro] retailer in the country was a Los Angeles Pep Boys [auto parts] store. . . . We discovered that the store was located just down the street from Universal Studios, and that the production guys were coming in and buying GoPro cameras by the dozens to use as crash cams and to capture [points of view] that were never before possible.[26]

In 2013 GoPros were so valued by TV producers that the company won a Technology and Engineering Emmy Award for the HERO3. Mark Burnett, famed producer of the *Survivor* TV show, explained why GoPro deserved the Emmy: "GoPro has allowed us to capture and share fascinating new perspectives that previously weren't possible . . . which in the end makes for better story telling."[27]

By 2014 the GoPro HERO had 4K capabilities, and point-of-view shots taken with the cameras were seen in reality TV shows,

RED cameras capture ultra-high-definition images but are smaller, lighter, and cheaper than traditional film cameras. In 2015 some of Hollywood's biggest movies, including The Martian (pictured), were shot using RED cameras.

independent films, and a few Hollywood blockbusters. GoPros were used to film a skydiving scene in *Captain Phillips* (2013), and the wearable cameras were used to capture daring stunts in *Fast & Furious 7* (2015).

While GoPros have been used for stunts, the 2015 blockbuster *The Martian* was the first to use the wearable camera in major scenes. In the film, Matt Damon portrays an astronaut stranded on Mars. According to the director, Ridley Scott, the GoPro was an important filmmaking tool:

> We used GoPro cameras in several of our biggest scenes in *The Martian*, and they really allowed us to capture not only the intensity and suspense of these moments, but also the intimacy of the characters themselves. New technologies like GoPro give filmmakers the opportunity to really push the language of cinema forward and introduce audiences to new perspectives and layers of storytelling that can really be quite engaging.[28]

Eye in the Sky

When GoPros are combined with drones, moviegoers can see eye-in-the-sky scenes that were impossible to shoot only a few years ago. Typical drones are about the size of a backpack. They are known as quadcopters because they use four whirling blades to fly.

Drone controls are easy to use, similar to those that operate remote-controlled cars. And filmmaking drones can carry cinema cameras that weigh up to 22 pounds (10 kg) at speeds of up to 40 miles per hour (64 kph).

quadcopter

A helicopter or drone lifted and propelled by four rotors.

Drones are nimble and cheap; the type of drone used in filmmaking is only about $1,000. In addition, drones save money for Hollywood filmmakers. Whereas a traditional shot with a helicopter and crew costs about $25,000 a day, the same shot using a drone handled by a trained pilot and professional camera operator costs about $5,000. Drones are also able to capture footage that would be difficult or impossible to obtain any other way. For example, when the Bardarbunga Volcano was in its early stages of eruption in Iceland in September 2014, the temperature above the molten lava was 2,100°F (1,149°C). This environment was far too dangerous to be approached by a film crew or helicopter. But videographer Eric Cheng believed he could fly a drone close enough to the volcano to grab some exciting movie footage with his GoPro HERO4 camera. The HERO4 is shockproof and waterproof, weighs a little over 3 ounces (85 grams), and shoots 4K video.

Cheng flew his drone-mounted GoPro 380 feet (116 m) above the volcano, and the footage looks like a CGI scene from a disaster movie. There were technical problems when the heat of the volcano eventually melted the face of the HERO4. But the camera's flash card preserved the one-of-a-kind shots of the bubbling, boiling lava, including explosions of red-hot magma shooting hundreds of feet into the air.

In 2015 so many amazing drone films like Cheng's were being made that director Randy Scott Slavin decided to start the

Superman with a GoPro

Drones equipped with GoPro cameras are allowing filmmakers to go where no camera has gone before. And filmmakers are expressing themselves with GoPros and drones in ways that would have been impossible only a few years ago. While some use their GoPros to soar above forests or volcanoes, filmmakers Sam Gorski and Niko Pueringer decided to show Superman's point of view as he zipped through the skies of Los Angeles.

Gorski and Pueringer used a GoPro drone to fly down the Los Angeles River and high above the city's freeways. Viewers can see the footage with a pair of outstretched Superman arms at the bottom of the frame. Other scenes were shot on the ground with actors, such as Superman stopping a robbery and saving a damsel in distress. *Superman with a GoPro* was an instant hit on YouTube, attracting 5 million views in just two days. Production partner Jake Watson described the motivation behind *Superman with a GoPro*: "We wanted to shoot a video with drones because it's new technology we're huge advocates of and have sort of made a living off shooting high-quality videos on a low budget, and we can't afford helicopters."

Quoted in Lindsay Deutsch, "Superman Soars Above L.A. with Drone Technology," *USA Today*, March 20, 2014. www.usatoday.com.

New York City Drone Film Festival. Tickets sold out within days for the first-ever festival of its kind. Attendees were able to see 35 drone films selected from 152 submissions. Many of the movies were experimental, made to demonstrate the abilities of the drone operator and the equipment. But as Slavin says, "the films that were shown were exceptional and amazing in different ways. When there is great storytelling and beautiful shots of landscapes or places you've never seen before, these films are just an amazing cross-section of possibilities. . . . Once Hollywood uses drones more, we're gonna see a lot more exciting scenes in general."[29]

A drone equipped with a GoPro camera flies over the Bardarbunga Volcano in Iceland as it erupts. Drones are able to capture footage that would be difficult or impossible to obtain any other way.

iPhone Films

Filmmakers can use GoPros because they produce high-quality 4K images. Although most smartphones do not have 4K capabilities, some filmmakers are using their iPhones to make movies. In 2015 John Lasseter, chief creative officer of Walt Disney Animation Studios, commented on the way small cameras are changing the way films look and feel: "The Go-pro and the iPhone are here. They give a vibrancy you have never been able to have before. . . . I think a new film [language] is going to come with these things."[30]

Lasseter gave his speech several weeks after the film *Tangerine* was shown at the prestigious Sundance Film Festival in Utah. *Tangerine*'s writer and director, Sean Baker, shot the entire movie on an iPhone 5s. Although amateur films are shot with iPhones every day, *Tangerine* was the first to debut at Sundance.

The film is a comedy-drama about three transgender hustlers living in a run-down Los Angeles neighborhood. Baker and his crew used three iPhones running an eight-dollar app called FiLMiC Pro. Each camera had a special lens attachment called an anamorphic adapter lens. When paired with an iPhone, the lens creates compelling video images that can be shown on a big screen.

Filming on a Shoestring Budget

The light, easy-to-operate iPhone allowed Baker to shoot *Tangerine* using innovative methods. He shot several scenes riding his bicycle in circles around the actors. Despite the low-budget techniques used to make the film, reviewers loved *Tangerine*. The film was nominated for numerous awards, and the reviews aggregator Rotten Tomatoes reported that *Tangerine* received almost unanimously positive reviews.

> **anamorphic**
>
> In filmmaking, the technique of shooting a widescreen picture with a non-widescreen camera such as a smartphone.

Baker believes anyone can create a film the way he did. But he points out that it takes more than an iPhone to win awards: "You still need to know how editing works. You still need to know how sound works. You still need to know how a camera works. . . . Yes, you can make a beautiful-looking film on a shoestring budget. But you have to know 100 years worth of filmmaking."[31]

Several other well-received films have been shot with iPhones, and there is little doubt that the ubiquitous smartphones are changing the way movies are made. The cameras are so lightweight and easy to use that films can be made quickly and cheaply; the well-received 2015 film *Uneasy Lies the Mind* was shot on an iPhone for a mere $10,000.

Virtual Reality

While smartphones are simplifying the moviemaking process, the devices are also being used to watch virtual reality films for

Virtual Reality: From Theory to Application

Virtual reality headsets went on sale for the first time in 2016, but the theory of VR goes back to 1968, when Dutch electronics firm Philips developed a head-mounted display called Headsight. The device, used for training helicopter pilots, was designed to simulate flying at night. Computer scientist Jaron Lanier coined the term *virtual reality* in 1987. Lanier was the cofounder of VPL Research, which developed products called the DataGlove and the EyePhone, virtual reality gloves and a headset. Both products were commercial failures. In the twenty-first century, virtual reality was largely ignored by the general public until 2014, when Facebook founder Mark Zuckerberg paid $2 billion to buy VR equipment maker Oculus from Palmer Luckey, who designed the Rift VR headset at the University of Southern California Institute for Creative Technologies. The publicity surrounding the Zuckerberg purchase spawned countless articles calling VR the next big thing. This helped attract widespread interest in virtual reality from gamers, filmmakers, and others.

the first time. One of the most innovative VR viewing platforms, Google Cardboard, works with any smartphone. Introduced in 2014, Cardboard is a simple, cardboard mount that holds a smartphone running the Cardboard app. Like VR headsets, the app provides two video images, one for each eye. This creates 3D images that provide a wide field of view similar to a virtual reality headset. Google does not manufacture Cardboard but makes a list of parts, plans, and assembly instructions available on its website. Users can assemble Cardboard for less than five dollars or purchase one made by independent manufacturers for less than thirty dollars.

In May 2015 Google released Jump, a camera rig for those who wish to make their own VR movies for viewing with Cardboard. The circular rig holds sixteen small cameras and captures 360 degrees of content, which lets viewers experience a scene from every direction. Jump software allows moviemakers to assemble the images into a film that can be viewed using Google Cardboard or any other VR headset. Jump software also works with the GoPro Odyssey, a $15,000 virtual reality rig outfitted with sixteen HERO4 cameras.

Virtual reality cameras are only one expense in the process of making 360-degree movies. Producers need powerful computers, scanners, and editing software to tackle the time-consuming process of making this type of movie. But the technology is going to change the way movies are made and seen in the future, as VR software developer Philip Lunn explains: "It's going to take time for [this new technology] to filter through. But it's kind of like the Wild West of computer graphics and filmmaking all over again, because people are trying to figure out a new thing. . . . The rules are different. We're going to experience and design things differently. We're going to visualize things differently. . . . It's such a fundamental shift."[32]

A new generation is embracing the changing rules and fundamental shifts driven by the latest cutting edge movie technology. The widespread availability of high-quality, compact digital cameras is opening doors for filmmakers of nearly every social status who want to tell their stories from their own unique viewpoints. Futurist Faith Popcorn explains how this trend will change Hollywood: "Bored with . . . the same millionaire directors, overexposed actors and predictable story lines, expect like-minded [moviemakers] to connect to create visions of their own. These . . . [films] will get widespread release, putting a much more democratic spin on the movie experience."[33] This shift will shake up Hollywood as the latest technology provides new possibilities for filmmakers, film watchers, and anyone with a smartphone and a good idea.

CHAPTER FOUR

Toys and Games

Kids growing up in the 1980s and 1990s could scarcely imagine the high-tech toys and games that are transforming the way people play. Virtual reality video games, autonomous robots, and 3D printed toys are just some of the gadgets on the horizon. Although many of the latest cutting edge toys and games are expensive, prices will come down as the technology becomes more common. Palmer Luckey, who invented the Oculus VR headset, explains: "[I] want to make VR cheap [and] functional. . . . Eventually, VR is going to run on every computer sold, and there will be a wide range of hardware at various price and quality points, a lot like televisions or monitors."[34]

Some high-tech toy makers are focusing on more than play. There is a growing demand for toys that teach STEM topics: science, technology, engineering, and math. This is unleashing a torrent of toys that encourage kids to build, invent, and experiment with circuits, lights, sensors, and motors. STEM-themed toys allow users to build robots, rockets, and drones. The Robot Turtles board game, invented by a Google engineer, even teaches kids ages three and up the basics of writing computer code.

Some educators want to turn STEM toys into STREAM toys by adding two other elements—reading and the arts. STREAM toys foster a sense of creativity by encouraging budding artists, music composers, and writers.

High-Tech Fun

The latest toy trends are even influencing the way old-school favorites are made. Lionel Trains, first sold in 1900, can now be controlled with a smartphone or tablet app. Even the traditional Crayola crayons have gone high-tech; Crayola's *Color Alive* app uploads pictures from coloring books to tablets. Users can add animation to bring the drawings to life.

Perhaps the biggest change in playtime is the move toward immersive environments. A new generation of small projectors can shine animated games onto a floor or wall. For the first time, any room can be turned into an interactive play space. Virtual reality headsets that transport users to alternative digital universes are changing the way video games are played.

Design and Create Toys

In 2016 one way STREAM topics were linked to playtime involved the use of 3D printers to design and produce toys. 3D printers make solid three-dimensional objects from a fine plastic dust called PMMA. The machines can be as small as a handheld pen or large enough to "print" a small automobile body.

Toy maker Mattel, famous for its Barbie dolls and Matchbox cars, is betting that the 3D toy trend is going to explode. In 2015 Mattel teamed with Autodesk, which specializes in 3D software for construction and manufacturing. According to Mattel, the two companies joined forces to "create the future of play."[35]

In this vision of the future, kids will use 3D software apps supplied by Mattel to design toys. These will be individually customized based on the user's own ideas and plans. For example, consumers will be able to make and print their own completely unique Barbie accessories or Hot Wheels cars. And if there is no 3D printer at home, kids can have the toys produced by a commercial printing facility. Mattel vice president Doug Wadleigh explains the company's move into consumer 3D toy printing: "We're constantly inspired by the passion and creativity we see among kids around the world. Technology is changing daily and . . . we're able to offer a new kind of 3D design experience, continuing the Mattel legacy of inspiring imagination and creativity."[36]

3D technology is also the driving force behind Cannybots, a series of smart robots that teach kids about computer programming, made by a British company of the same name. Cannybots offers 3D-printable Bluetooth-enabled toy cars that can be controlled with smartphones or tablets. The Cannybots construction kit includes an app called *Canny Talk*, which allows users to program the robots using plain English. For example, users can make the cars move in patterns with simple commands such as "turn right" and "move forward." Kids can make a track for the Cannybots using black electrical tape or create a custom track on a 3D printer. Cannybots CEO Anish Mampetta explains the concept: "Going through the building process gives kids the hands-on experience of building a functional robot that they can also program. Programming is an essential skill today but it is not easy to get kids started. We are allowing kids to do this in a fun, interactive and rewarding way."[37]

Dogs and Droids

Those who did not wish to build their own toys could buy a range of complex robots and droids in 2016. A company called WowWee Robotics introduced a robot dog named ChiP (Canine Home Intelligent Pet). The $199 robot is infused with artificial intelligence (AI), which means the internal computer in ChiP can execute tasks that normally require human intelligence. For example, ChiP recognizes its owner and responds to commands. Like all dogs, ChiP can play fetch, but the robot dog also plays soccer. When ChiP is tired—or running low on power—the robot dog will head to its bed to get recharged. And unlike other dogs, ChiP navigates the world with GPS and avoids running into things using infrared sensors that allow the robot to "see" objects and stairs.

While ChiP is recharging, robot fans can play with WowWee's AI robotic battle game R.E.V. AIR. The game takes its name from its parts—a Robotic Enhanced Vehicle (R.E.V) and AIR quadcopter drone. Both pieces fire virtual missiles, and both can move autonomously (on their own) or be controlled by a smartphone app.

autonomous

Free to act independently.

The *Star Wars* films have been inspiring robot toys since the late 1970s. But the toy based on the BB-8 droid in *Star Wars VII: The Force Awakens* (2015) was one of the most advanced. The BB-8 droid toy from Sphero interacts with a smartphone app that allows users to steer it, talk to it, and send it video messages. BB-8 also acts autonomously when put in "patrol" mode; the droid wanders around a room and keeps data on possible boundaries and obstacles to avoid collisions. Additionally, BB-8 can be controlled by a Force Band worn on the wrist. Users sweep their arms right, left, backward, or forward to move the droid about.

The BB-8 toy, based on the droid from Star Wars VII: The Force Awakens, is one of the most advanced robot toys available. Users can control BB-8 with a smartphone app or by wearing a Force Band, enabling them to move the droid about with Jedi-like movements.

The Real Cost of Virtual Reality

When the first Rift VR headsets were made available for preorder in January 2016, so many people visited the Oculus website that it nearly crashed. Although consumers were eager to get hold of the latest trend in gaming and movie viewing, first-generation VR headsets had a few glitches: They were expensive and clunky, and they required extra equipment.

The first-generation PlayStation VR cost $1,200, about three times more than the PlayStation 4. At a cost of $600, the Oculus Rift was also expensive. Additionally, the headset was not a standalone device; the Rift could only be used with high-end Oculus-certified PCs that had about three times the processing power of average computers sold in 2015. The upgraded PCs added an extra $1,500 to $2,000 to the price of using a Rift VR.

Some early users say that cost is not the only problem. A number of reviewers say that VR headsets are clunky because of the long wires attached to them. As tech reviewer Ben Gilbert explains: "If you stand up and walk around, the wires are only so long and, ya know, you've got a big headset on blocking your entire field of vision. You . . . might knock over your computer or game console!" Additionally, the VR headsets come with external cameras and sensors that must be mounted in the room where they are used. The sensors record the movements of the user from the outside and translate the actions to the headset, which changes the view accordingly.

Ben Gilbert, "6 Things You Should Know Before Buying a Virtual Reality Headset," *Tech Insider*, January 7, 2016. www.techinsider.io.

New Wave of Video Games

While autonomous robots have been shaking up the toy industry, video game creators are hoping virtual reality will be a major game changer. And video games are among the first entertainment options offered for VR headsets like the Oculus Rift and the HTC Vive. The Sony PlayStation VR is the first virtual reality game console.

Virtual reality places a vast 3D video game in front of the users' eyes. The headsets work with motion controllers that play an important role in the VR experience by providing a sense of having hands in the virtual world. Depending on the game, hand controllers let a user grip a virtual Ping-Pong paddle, hold a sword, sculpt and paint a masterpiece, or perform dozens of other tasks. Oculus Rift works with a pair of VR controllers called Oculus Touch. Each handheld Oculus Touch grip holds buttons and sensors that translate the motions of the fingers, hands, and arms to the virtual space. The controllers also provide tactile feedback; they allow users to feel the virtual objects they pick up.

The VR hardware company Leap Motion allows users to play without handheld controllers. The Leap is a small device that hooks onto the front of a VR headset. It has a camera and motion sensors that track users' hand movements so they can be seen on the VR screen.

Some developers are making other equipment to enhance the VR experience for users who wander far and wide in virtual worlds. In 2016 a company called 3DRudder introduced a foot-based VR motion device. Seated users rest their feet on the 3DRudder disc and tilt it forward to move forward. The disc also tilts backward and side to side, and it spins in any direction. 3DRudder can also be used to eliminate the joystick in traditional video games. Tech reviewer Seth Colander explains why the 3DRudder improves a players' game: "If you can [change] your in-game movement from your two hands to your feet, that frees you up to use other input devices such as the hand controllers used by the Oculus Rift and HTC Vive for things like grabbing objects and firing weapons."[38]

omnidirectional

Working or existing in every direction.

A motion control device called ROVR is meant to allow players to move freely and unencumbered in the VR world. The ROVR is defined by the tongue-twisting term Virtual Reality Omnidirectional Locomotion Platform. Users stand on the ROVR platform and are held in place by a padded railing that encircles the device. Rather than walk, users change their foot positions by sliding the feet back and forth. Locomotion platforms like the ROVR are seen as exciting additions to virtual reality because they translate a user's movements into walking, running, leaping,

In 2016 a company called 3DRudder introduced a foot-based VR motion device (pictured), which allows seated users hands-free movement through VR environments. The disc can also be used to eliminate the joystick in traditional video games.

snowboarding, skateboarding, or climbing stairs, depending on the game.

Another VR accessory is aimed at those who want to exercise while playing. A company called VirZOOM created wireless sensors that are attached to a stationary bicycle. The sensors connect to a VR headset and allow the player to interact with the game. Tech reviewer Lily Prasuethsut took the VR bike for a spin: "The demo on hand involved riding a horse which could turn into a [flying horse] Pegasus if you find wings and then pedaled faster. Being a horse while pedaling is jarring at first but really fun once you get the hang of it."[39] VirZOOM has been working to expand its concept to let players assume the form of dragons, tanks, and other objects.

Expanding the Sandbox

Virtual reality is a perfect medium for open-world, or sandbox, games, which allow users to wander vast landscapes for hours at a time. In 2016 some of the best-selling video games were sandbox games, including *Destiny*, *Minecraft*, and *Grand Theft Auto V*. (The term *sandbox* traces its history to the original *Minecraft*, which provided users with a giant sandpit waiting to be molded into fortresses and other objects.) The most advanced sandbox games have gigantic playing fields, or maps, filled with characters, shops, and other things players can interact with.

sandbox

Also known as open world, a type of video game in which players can roam freely to complete missions and objectives.

The sandbox games made today have much bigger maps than those created in the mid-2000s. For example, in 2006 the role-playing fantasy video game *Elder Scrolls IV* gave users 16 square miles (41 sq km) to roam around in. In 2014 the military game *ArmA3*, which depicts a conflict on a fictional island called Altis, had a playing field of 104 square miles (269 sq km). To put that in perspective, it can take a player seven hours of real time to walk across Altis.

Sandbox games are a natural match for full-immersion virtual reality, and developers are hard at work updating the latest games for VR headsets. In 2016 Microsoft announced that *Minecraft Windows 10 Edition* would be one of the first games available for the Oculus Rift and Gear VR. *Minecraft* is the third-best-selling PC game worldwide, with more than 70 million copies in circulation in 2015. John Carmack, legendary creator of *Doom* and chief technology officer at Oculus, believes that more people will purchase expensive VR headsets just to play *Minecraft*: "I think [*Minecraft* is] the single most important application that we can do for virtual reality, to make sure that we have an army of fanatic, passionate supporters that will advocate why VR is great. . . . So this is . . . huge."[40]

Mind-Control VR Gaming

Companies are competing to create new and better control devices for VR gaming, including hand and foot controllers and even wired-up stationary bikes. But in 2015 a Swiss medical device company called MindMaze unveiled an invention that will free players from physical controllers. MindLeap is the world's first thought-powered virtual reality game system.

MindLeap features a virtual reality headset attached to a rope and plastic net that covers the crown of the head. The net contains electroencephalograph (EEG) sensors that record electrical activity within the brain. In recent years EEG sensors have been incorporated into artificial limbs to allow users to control the devices with their thought. With the MindLeap, the sensors allow users to conduct thought-driven game play.

Tech reviewer Adi Robertson used MindLeap to play a simple sphere-themed fighting game using only her thoughts: "Each player is represented by a glowing sphere, trying to push a smaller ball into the opponent. To build up power and defend against attacks, you relax, letting your mind go blank. . . . To attack, you frown, furrowing your brow cartoonishly and staring hard." Although MindLeap can read simple thoughts of relaxation and anger, the device is not developed enough to allow complex actions. But in the future, users might play games like *Grand Theft Auto* using only their brain waves.

Adi Robertson, "MindMaze's Hand-Tracking, Mind-Reading Virtual Reality Headset Is Just as Complicated as It Sounds," Verge, March 4, 2015. www.theverge.com.

Other popular games are being expanded to appeal to that army of passionate VR gamers. *Battlezone*, first introduced as an Atari arcade game in 1980, is being remade for modern VR headsets. Another game, *Super Hypercube*, is a VR version of the best-selling *Tetris* puzzle game. *Super Hypercube* allows players to twist blocks in a 3D space to fit through shifting holes in a wall.

Dreams of the Future

In 2016 other VR games helped shine a light on the future of gaming. Sony's *Eve: Valkyrie* is a highly polished space combat game that put gamers in command of a heavily armed fighter engaged in realistic dogfights. *Dreams*, one of the most original concepts for VR sandbox gaming, allows users to recreate their dreams in 3D using tactile gamepad tools. *Dreams* players can pick environments, characters, props, toys, and tools. *Wired* editor Michael Rundle describes the game and its unique possibilities:

> You can start with a sphere, pop holes for eyes with the corner of a cube, and carve out a grinning mouth yourself, or you can drop pre-made trees, houses, jetpacks or thousands of other objects directly into the scene. . . . When uploaded [players'] dreams will form self-contained, shareable game worlds. . . . Watching *Dreams* in action, it's obvious that the ease of use will open up immediate creative possibilities—and might lead to a community with a genuinely hallucinatory and unique creative energy [41]

VR Headaches

For some, the dream of virtual reality can turn into a nightmare; the headsets can cause physical problems and—some say—psychological harm. In the physical realm, VR headsets can cause dizziness, fatigue, and nausea from motion sickness for people who wear them as they move around while playing games. This is due to what designers call latency. This is the lag time between the physical turning of the head and the time it takes for that movement to be registered on the VR display. If the latency is longer than a few milliseconds, the user can become ill.

Virtual reality headsets can also cause problems for about one in four thousand people who experience dizziness, seizures, or blackouts when exposed to certain patterns of flashing lights. According to the health and safety warnings accompanying the Rift VR, the headsets can cause problems even in people who have never before experienced blackouts or seizures. Because of the possible dangers of VR headsets, the restaurant chain Chuck E. Cheese's removed the *Ticket Blaster* virtual reality game from its locations in 2014.

Augmented Reality

People who fear the risks of virtual reality might want to try augmented reality (AR). Augmented reality relies on devices that look like glasses or goggles to blend digital content into the real world. These devices provide what is called a heads-up display, digital information that can be seen without looking down or lowering the eyes. With a heads-up display, the wearer looks at the real world while AR glasses add graphics, sounds, and tactile feedback to the natural world as it exists. The Virtual Reality Site explains the difference between AR and VR: "Whereas virtual reality immerses your senses completely in a world that only exists in the digital realm, augmented reality takes the real world of the present and projects digital imagery and sound into it."[42]

> **augmented**
>
> **Made better or different by having been added to.**

Augmented reality glasses rely on extremely complex technology. At the most basic level, AR glasses use a camera to examine the surrounding world. The images are wirelessly transferred to GPS software that pinpoints the user's position and pulls relevant data about the location from the Internet. Various apps interpret the information and divide it into categories such as driving directions, businesses, museums, and so on. A tiny internal projector displays the information on the lens of the AR glasses. For example, a user might look at a restaurant and see the menu displayed in the corner of screen. An external projector can display the information onto a wall, hand, or other surface in front of the wearer.

Users can control AR glasses in various ways. The goggles can track eye movements, such as blinks, to perform a certain task; blink twice to take a picture, for example. The glasses also listen to voice commands and follow hand gestures. Microsoft makes a set of AR glasses called HoloLens. Tech analyst Patrick Moorhead describes using the HoloLens to fix a light switch: "I was installing a dimmer switch on a wall, and I had a person on Skype on the right-hand side of my screen walking me through exactly how to do it. And because they could see what I'm seeing as well, they could . . . use a green pen to mark the right wires to connect, or point me to which tools I should pick up."[43]

AR Gaming

In 2016 augmented reality was one of the hottest trends in gaming. Microsoft created an AR version of *Minecraft*. Players wearing the HoloLens can see all the *Minecraft* buildings and characters on the furniture in their living room. The AR software incorporates the room into the scene so players can interact with the game as they walk around. Moorhead describes his *Minecraft* AR experience: "One of the neatest scenes involved me setting off TNT on top of the table, which blew a virtual hole in it, and I could see into the hole to where characters had fallen into virtual molten lava."[44]

Augmented reality is also being incorporated into other popular games. *Human Pac-Man* is based on the popular *Pac-Man* arcade game of the 1980s. The new version lets users chase after one another while the AR glasses make opponents look like *Pac-Man* characters.

Some tech analysts believe that by 2020, people will be playing augmented reality games in the streets. Scavenger hunts will be conducted with players who use their AR glasses to find virtual objects. And the glasses will also have a use as tools for what is called "edutainment" (educational entertainment). Users will be able to beam the planets of the solar system on the wall or create 3D scenes from Shakespeare plays. Augmented reality could also be used to show people how to cook, play an instrument, or knit a sweater.

With the introduction of Oculus Rift, PlayStation VR, and a range of high-tech toys, 2016 will be remembered as year one in the virtual revolution. And the new digital realities will likely affect society on all levels. The devices will not just change the way people play but also the way they interact with the world while working, traveling, and learning. As the walls break down between the digital and real domains, the sandbox expands every day, and the possibilities seem as endless as a player's dreams.

CHAPTER FIVE

Museums and Theme Parks

Museums and theme parks around the world attract millions of visitors each year. In 2014 more than 107 million people visited the world's top twenty museums—among them the Louvre in Paris, the Metropolitan Museum of Art in New York City, and the Smithsonian National Air and Space Museum in Washington, DC. Theme parks were even more popular. More than 223 million visited the top twenty theme parks—among them Universal Studios in Florida and California and Disneyland theme parks worldwide. Interest in both museums and theme parks continues to grow. Worldwide museum attendance was up nearly 2 percent in 2014 from the previous year, and theme park attendance grew by 4 percent.

To remain relevant and keep attendance growing, museums and theme parks have to balance beloved traditions with new and exciting features. For example, parents who went to Disneyland in their youth may want their kids to try out the same rides they once enjoyed. But kids also want to take the newest rides based on the latest movie or video game. Museums also need to grow and change to stay relevant. Although museums might exhibit ancient artworks and historical artifacts, the institutions also need to attract young generations raised on smartphones and the Internet. To blend the old with the new, museums and theme parks are using augmented reality and virtual reality to engage and entertain guests.

Art Museums of the Future

In some circles art museums have a reputation for being old-fashioned institutions filled with dusty works and musty antiques. Small tags called didactic panels display some information about a work of art but often provide little context about their history or creation. Art museum curators believe the experience can be greatly enhanced by placing interactive digital display panels near works of art. These displays, perhaps combined with augmented reality goggles, would reveal information about a work's creator, history, art genre, and other facts. Museum specialist Craig Hanna imagines a heads-up AR display integrated into a clear display case in front of each piece of art:

Through the display, the guest can explore the history of the object, the tools and techniques used to create it, the historical timelines that parallel its creation. With the wave of a hand a patron can learn more about the artist, link to other works that have a significant connection, grab a virtual magnifying glass and drag it across the canvas to "see" the brush work up close, or open video clips [with] interesting information about the item. They can even record and share their own insights about the item for others to access.[45]

Although advanced heads-up displays are not yet available, museums are working to integrate touch screens into exhibits. The *Mummies* exhibit at the Natural History Museum in Los Angeles has touch screen tables that allow users to digitally unwrap the mummies on display while learning about life in ancient Egypt. The Cleveland Museum of Art features a 40-foot (12 m) touch screen *Collection Wall*. This interactive display allows patrons to learn about and view all forty-two hundred works of art in the museum's permanent collection.

Tailor-Made Experiences

Heads-up displays would work with audio feeds to improve the museum experience. The audio guides would go beyond the familiar headphones once worn by patrons who listened to dry facts

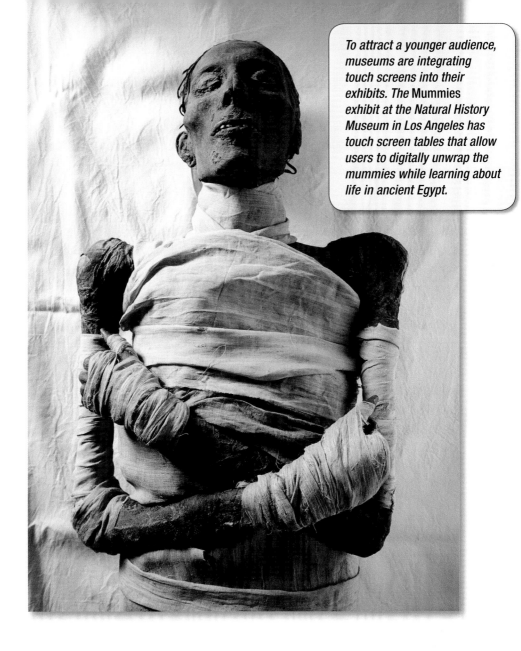

To attract a younger audience, museums are integrating touch screens into their exhibits. The Mummies exhibit at the Natural History Museum in Los Angeles has touch screen tables that allow users to digitally unwrap the mummies while learning about life in ancient Egypt.

and figures about exhibits on clunky cassette players. The audio tours of the future will be much more interactive, with a variety of people with different perspectives adding their personal views about a piece of art. Commentary might feature humor, sarcasm, or opposing viewpoints. Patrons would be able to record their own views, like a comments section on a website.

The Broad Museum in Los Angeles is already offering an expanded audio experience. Tiny Bluetooth beacons positioned

Projecting an Artistic Message

Augmented reality is the latest trend among museum curators, but artists are also using AR technology beyond museum walls. Phoenix artists Lauren Strohacker and Kendra Sollars use large-format HD projectors to display images of vanishing native species on the walls of urban environments. Visitors to downtown Phoenix might turn a corner and see ghostly blue-white images of two vultures 30 feet (9 m) high projected on the side of a building. The startling 3D images are meant to remind viewers that urban sprawl is displacing animals and destroying their natural habitat. The artists have also displayed Mexican wolf silhouettes on Tucson buildings and mule deer in a vacant Phoenix lot. As Sollars explains: "Whatever space or city we're in, we try to [project] animals native to the area. It's very site-specific. . . . It's interesting to see how many people don't recognize native species. It really plays into that ecological loss."

The type of HD projectors used by Strohacker and Sollars are also used to provide dazzling backdrops and shifting scenery on theme park rides. The high-tech projectors can change the look and feel of a setting in seconds, and the possibilities are only limited by the imagination.

Quoted in Liesl Bradner, "'Animal Land' Art Project Puts Vanishing Native Species in Perspective," *Los Angeles Times*, January 9, 2016. www.latimes.com.

around the galleries direct headphone-wearing visitors to points of interest. Each point has its own audio guide. A guide aimed at children is narrated by LeVar Burton, the long-running host of the PBS children's series *Reading Rainbow*. Another guide features well-known artists talking about their favorite works by other artists. For example, renowned sculptor Jeff Koons comments on the pop art paintings of Roy Lichtenstein.

The move toward interactive audio is meant to appeal to the desires of patrons raised in a selfie culture. As MuseumNext founder Jim Richardson explains: "I think the future of museums will be a lot more personalized than the current one-fits-all visitor experience, with technology allowing people with different interests to each have a tailored experience."[46]

Whatever the advantages of advanced technology, high-tech gadgets can conflict with tradition. Not everyone wants to see blue glowing screens when they stand in front of iconic paintings and sculptures. As *Los Angeles Times* reporter Jessica Gelt explains: "For every app-loving, gadget-embracing museum curator or visitor there is a solitude-craving, analog enthusiast who feels that pixelated screens and interactive devices interfere with the very soul of the museum-going experience. Their goal is to stand quietly in front of art and ponder its significance and place in history—without technological intrusion."[47]

curator

A person who manages and looks after artwork in a museum.

Blending Old and New

The intrusion of technology is the point of augmented reality, and some museums have already started using AR to provide interactive history lessons. Museums in Amsterdam, Chicago, and London now offer free AR smartphone apps that interact with photo and painting collections. In 2016 visitors in London could use the *Streetmuseum* app provided by the Museum of London. The app guides users to select buildings and street corners in the city. A tap on the screen brings up a historic photo of the site. The app also provides a description of the location, the date the original image was created, and the photographer's name.

Users can hold their camera phone up to the modern location and click "3D view" on *Streetmuseum*. This action prompts the app to overlay the historic image over part of the view, augmenting the reality displayed on the smartphone screen. For example, a person standing on the Tower Bridge over the Thames River can see the steel-and-glass buildings of modern London on the right side of the smartphone screen. On the left a black-and-white photograph taken in 1930 by George Davison Reid shows the ships and buildings of old London wreathed in fog.

Visitors to the Smithsonian National Museum of Natural History in Washington, DC, can mix the very old with the new using another AR option. The Smithsonian's Bone Hall, opened in 1881, holds more than three hundred dinosaur skeletons. Visitors can download the free *Skin & Bones* app, which uses 3D augmented-reality technology to bring the dinosaurs to life. Visitors who hold their smartphones up to dinosaur skeletons can see how the animals looked when they were alive, how they moved, and how their skeletons moved. When a phone is pointed at the skull of a diamondback rattlesnake, users can watch it sink its long fangs into a virtual rodent.

Videos linked to the *Skin & Bones* app show Smithsonian scientists discussing topics such as ecology and evolution. According to museum outreach program manager Robert Costello: "From vampire bats to a 150-pound Mississippi catfish, 'Skin and Bones'

Visitors to the Smithsonian in Washington, DC, can download the Skin & Bones app, which uses AR technology to bring dinosaurs to life. By holding their smartphones up to dinosaur skeletons like the one pictured here, visitors can see how the animals looked and moved when they were alive.

highlights specimens across the tree of vertebrate life and invites visitors to interact with them in surprising ways."[48]

Theme Park of the Future

The idea of fusing excitement, education, and virtual reality is a hot trend in the other branch of the attractions industry, theme parks. In 2015 the Los Angeles–based Landmark Entertainment Group announced it would break ground on a virtual reality theme park at an as-yet-unspecified location in China by 2017. The park will be called Landmark Interactive Virtual Experience, or L.I.V.E., Centre. It will include a digital art gallery, a virtual museum, a virtual zoo and aquarium, and VR rides and attractions.

animatronics

The technique of making and operating lifelike robots, typically for use in film or theme park entertainment.

Landmark is known for creating Universal Studios theme park attractions like Kongfrontation and the Amazing Adventures of Spider-Man 5D. The popular attractions thrill and entertain visitors using video projection, HD sound, tactile sensors, laser lights, and robotic creatures, or animatronics. These systems have been used in theme park attractions for more than a decade.

Landmark wants to move beyond traditional theme park entertainment systems by adding virtual reality. As Landmark CEO Tony Christopher explains:

> With virtual reality we can put you in the African savannah or fly you into outer space. This completely changes the idea of an old-fashioned museum by allowing kids to experience prehistoric dinosaurs or legendary creatures. . . . We'll combine education and entertainment into one destination that's always evolving. . . . [And] we're already thinking about how VR and alternate reality can create the theme park of the future.[49]

Christopher believes L.I.V.E. Centre visitors will be excited and frightened when they see lifelike dinosaurs in their VR headsets and hear the beasts roaring in their ears. Theme park fans of the future will not have to travel to China for this experience. Landmark plans to build twenty to thirty L.I.V.E. Centre theme parks throughout the world by 2025.

Coasting to New Heights

The types of rides that will be offered at the L.I.V.E. Centre were not announced. But ride engineers are working on the next generation of amusement park attractions. Much of the focus is centered on one of the most popular thrill rides, the roller coaster.

Designers of roller coasters are sometimes compared to mad scientists because the rides seem to get faster and scarier every year. Two examples of record-breaking roller-coaster madness were expected to open in 2016. The Joker at California's Six Flags Discovery Kingdom is named after the Batman villain. The coaster makes riders feel weightless with a zero-gravity barrel roll. After a frighteningly steep 78-degree drop, the Joker flips passengers horizontally in what Six Flags calls the world's first "step-up under-flip inverted roll."[50]

zero gravity

A condition in which there is no apparent force of gravity acting on a body.

Not to be outdone, Cedar Point in Sandusky, Ohio, expected to open the Valravn ride in 2016. The coaster is named after a supernatural bird from Danish legend. According to Cedar Point, the Valravn is the "tallest, fastest, longest dive coaster in the world."[51] The ride includes a free fall with a 90-degree drop—straight down for 214 feet (65 m) at speeds reaching 75 miles per hour (121 kph). The Valravn will shatter ten world records, including tallest, fastest, and longest dive coaster; most inversions; and longest drop.

While some roller-coaster designers continue to push the envelope, others want to combine the physical world with the digital universe. One day, virtual reality roller coasters may take passen-

Designing Attractions with VR

The newest attractions at Disney parks in California, Florida, Japan, and elsewhere are designed with virtual reality tools by a team of creative artists and engineers called Disney Imagineers. The Imagineers use VR to work out issues of scale, timing, animation, and sight lines for new rides, restaurants, and even hotel suites.

The work of the Imagineers takes place in a high-tech studio called the Digital Immersive Showroom (DISH) in Glendale, California. The room housing DISH is like a large soundstage used to film movies and television shows. It contains four high-definition projectors, which create a 3D environment for those wearing 3D glasses. Visitors to the DISH wear hats with sensors that track their head movements and adjust the 3D images accordingly. Travel writer Adrienne Vincent-Phoenix describes a VR ride on the proposed Car Land attraction:

> I was impressed by how completely my mind accepted the projected images as real physical items. While wearing the hat, I could walk around and even between items in the image as if they were really there, bend down to examine detail, then look to the horizon and watch the sight lines change as I moved about. The effect is convincing enough that . . . I was careful not to step into the virtual gas pump my brain insisted was still really behind me.

Adrienne Vincent-Phoenix, "Step into the DISH—A Visit to Imagineering's Digital Immersive Showroom," Mouse Planet, June 5, 2012. www.mouseplanet.com.

gers to fictional fantasy lands while their bodies experience the movements of actual roller coasters.

A company called VR Coaster designs virtual reality headsets that can be worn by roller-coaster passengers. The headsets present nonstop action in a 360-degree 3D setting. In one scenario, riders are accompanied by animated characters as they travel through a virtual cave. The roller coaster seems to be dodging falling rocks as it travels over bubbling pools of lava and crosses

The idea of fusing excitement and virtual reality is a hot trend in the theme park industry. One day in the near future virtual reality roller coasters may take passengers on rides to fictional fantasy lands.

dangerously swaying bridges. Other VR roller-coaster adventures feature a flying stagecoach pulled by winged horses and a journey on the back of a flying dragon. In 2016 the headsets were in the testing phase as engineers worked to sync the visuals on the screen with the drops, rolls, and gravitational forces provided by a real roller coaster.

Another company is hoping to offer an exhilarating coaster experience without the expense of actually building a roller coaster. The Rilix Coaster is a stationary vehicle that is synchronized with a virtual reality headset. The vehicle can be programmed from mild to wild; it rocks, twists, and turns depending on the passengers' tolerance level. Riders experience 3D visuals that include horror or science fiction scenes.

Gaming in the Void

In addition to putting riders in fantasy settings, theme parks are making plans to integrate popular video games into their attractions. In 2015 Nintendo was working with Universal to bring Donkey Kong, Mario, and the rest of the company's collection of characters to Nintendo-themed rides. But tech entrepreneur Ken Bretschneider hopes to take the video game concept to another level; he wants to meld virtual reality with physical gaming in a theme park setting.

Bretschneider is cofounder of the Void Virtual Entertainment Center (VEC), a theme park that was scheduled to open in Utah's Salt Lake City area in 2016. The VEC will provide a multiplayer VR experience in which six to eight people can play together on a 60-by-60-foot (18-by-18-m) stage. The stage will have walls, boxes, and other modules that can be moved around to offer players different types of exploration within the virtual world. For example, portable walls can be used to create a small maze that feels infinitely larger when combined with virtual visuals.

For large, multiplayer games, designers imagine players on multiple stages within a single park or connected to other VECs. For example, a VR Capture the Flag or science fiction shooter tournament could engage numerous players simultaneously at Void VECs throughout the country.

A Rival to Disney World

The Void experience adds special effects such as smells, heat, and surround sound to the visuals in the VR headset. One of the games designed for the experience is called *Ghost vs. Hunters*. The game takes place in a haunted house, where players try to capture ghosts by setting traps. The ghosts fight back, haunting the hunters by touching them or scaring them with loud noises, sprays of water, and foul smells. Designers believe that the haunted VR experience will be much more frightening than a traditional haunted house attraction at a theme park. As tech reviewer Dave Smith writes, the Void designers "are creating fun and innovative experiences that rival anything you'd see at Disney World or Universal Studios."[52]

Before visitors enter a stage at the Void, they will dress in custom-designed VR helmets that offer a 180-degree field of vision on a curved OLED screen. Players will wear vests that incorporate five tactile feedback sensors. These will produce numerous physical sensations that include getting shot and standing near an explosion. A pair of glove controllers will let players touch and interact with virtual objects. Rachel Metz, senior editor of *MIT Technology Review*, explains how this high-tech gear created a unique experience as she explored a virtual Mayan temple:

> I reach out to touch one of the crumbling stone walls on my left. . . . There appears to be a glowing torch on the wall; I reach out and feel something that could indeed be a torch, so I pick it up and use it to light my way as I wander down the dark passageways, inspecting carvings and statuary along the sides. . . . A fire burns in the middle of one passageway, and I actually feel its warmth on my face. At one point, standing in a cave on a rickety-looking platform overlooking an underground pool, I press my hand onto a small podium in front of me, and the platform rumbles and rises off the ground.[53]

"Changing and Morphing"

The Void is the ultimate in immersive virtual theme park entertainment. Planners and engineers expect theme park rides of the future to entertain in a similar manner. Guests will likely wear digital wristbands that allow them to have tailor-made, interactive experiences based on their personal preferences. This sort of futuristic entertainment is described by theme park planner Bill Bunting, who says that designers will create "rides that can recognize guests individually, and adapt the show experience for them in ways we have only begun to understand. Multiple ride paths, interactive [games], and on-demand . . . media will allow us to create rides that are constantly changing and morphing, encouraging repeat ridership like never before."[54]

With the never-ending need to keep guests coming through the turnstiles, amusement parks and museums will continue to change with the latest high-tech inventions. At the same time, the attractions industry will work to maintain its core mission—providing lasting memories for each generation of visitors. Those recollections might involve gazing in awe at a fifteenth-century painting with an AR overlay or dropping down a dive coaster while riding a flying dragon. The marriage of high-tech, amusement, and edutainment continues to evolve with the times.

Source Notes

Chapter One: Music and Concerts

1. Lucianne Walkowicz, "Rhythms of Starlight, Melodies of Astrophysics," *TED Blog*, March 8, 2013. http://blog.ted.com.
2. Walkowicz, "Rhythms of Starlight, Melodies of Astrophysics."
3. Dennis P. Paul, "An Instrument for the Sonification of Everyday Things," Vimeo, 2012. http://dennisppaul.de.
4. Paul, "An Instrument for the Sonification of Everyday Things."
5. Quoted in 98.7KLUV, "Neil Young Hates MP3 Quality, Says We're Missing 95% of the Sound!," January 26, 2012. http://kluv.cbslocal.com.
6. Quoted in David Pogue, "Neil Young's PonoPlayer: The Emperor Has No Clothes," Yahoo! Tech, January 29, 2015. www.yahoo.com.
7. Seth Stevenson, "Out of the Blue and into the Wack," *Slate*, February 20, 2015. www.slate.com.
8. Sierra Vandervort, "Yes, We Love EDM and No, We're Not All on Drugs," *Elite Daily*, August 22, 2014. http://elitedaily.com.
9. Peter Rubinstein, "The Use of Technology to Enhance Music Festivals," Your EDM, March 7, 2015. www.youredm.com.
10. Jelmer Tiete, "Tomorrowland Bracelet Teardown," J, November 17, 2014. http://jelmertiete.com.
11. Peter Rubenstein, "See TomorrowWorld in 360 Degree Full Party Immersion Technology," Your EDM, March 19, 2015. www.youredm.com.
12. Rubinstein, "See TomorrowWorld in 360 Degree Full Party Immersion Technology."

Chapter Two: Television Trends

13. Marcus Wohlsen, "As Online Viewing Soars, Internet TV Will Soon Be the Only TV," *Wired*, October 20, 2014. www.wired.com.

14. David Pierce, "Avegant's Glyph Headset Is a Movie Theater for Your Face," *Wired*, December 15, 2015. www.wired.com.

15. Quoted in Zoë Clapp, ed., *2014: The Future of Television*. London: Premium, 2014, p. 17.

16. Quoted in Clapp, *2014*, p. 17.

17. Quoted in Callie Bost, "MIT Researcher Says Holographic TV Could Debut in the Next 10 Years," Bloomberg Business, June 19, 2013. www.bloomberg.com.

18. Quoted in David S. Cohen, "Holographic Video: Not Just for the Jetsons Anymore," *Variety*, August 13, 2014. http://variety.com.

19. Quoted in *Wired*, "4-D Cinema Explores Shake, Rattle and Sniff Options," July 15, 2011. www.wired.com.

20. Quoted in Consumer Electronics Association, *Technology Trends to Watch 2015*. Arlington, VA: CEA, 2015, p. 20.

Chapter Three: Movies

21. Will Shanklin, "Samsung Gear VR Review: Almost an Oculus Rift, No PC Required," Gizmag, November 27, 2015. www.gizmag.com.

22. Steven Zeitchik, "Hollywood Looks to Bring Virtual-Reality Cinema to Life," *Los Angeles Times*, March 8, 2015. www.latimes.com.

23. Quoted in Zeitchik, "Hollywood Looks to Bring Virtual-Reality Cinema to Life."

24. Nick Pino, "4k TV and UHD: Everything You Need to Know About Ultra HD," TechRadar, January 25, 2016. www.techradar.com.

25. Nick Zurko, "How RED Cameras Changed the Game," New York Film Academy, August 7, 2015. www.nyfa.edu.

26. Quoted in GoPro, "And the Emmy Goes to . . . GoPro," 2016. https://gopro.com.

27. Quoted in GoPro, "And the Emmy Goes to . . . GoPro."

28. Quoted in GoPro, "Legendary Hollywood Director Ridley Scott Incorporates GoPro into the Making and Storyline of *The Martian*," October 1, 2015. http://investor.gopro.com.

29. Quoted in Alex Bracetti, "Interview: Randy Scott Slavin, Founder of the Worlds' First Drone Film Festival," Green Label, April, 16, 2015. http://greenlabel.com.
30. Quoted in James Rainey, "Pixar's John Lasseter Says iPhone, Go-Pro Could Be Next Film Breakthroughs," *Variety*, May 12, 2015. http://variety.com.
31. Quoted in Casey Newton, "How One of the Best Films at Sundance Was Shot Using an iPhone 5s," Verge, January 28, 2015. www.theverge.com.
32. Quoted in David Nield, "The Brave New World of Virtual-Reality Filmmaking," *ReadWrite*, June 25, 2015. http://readwrite.com.
33. Faith Popcorn, "The Future of Films," *Brainreserve* (blog), December 4, 2014. www.faithpopcorn.com.

Chapter Four: Toys and Games

34. Quoted in Matt Kamen, "Oculus Rift Will Get Cheaper, Says Palmer Luckey," *Wired*, January 11, 2016. www.wired.co.uk.
35. Quoted in Bridget Butler Millsaps, "Mattel and Autodesk Team Up to Bring World of Toy Customization Apps & 3D Printing to Kids," 3dPrint, April 20, 2015. http://3dprint.com.
36. Quoted in Millsaps, "Mattel and Autodesk Team Up to Bring World of Toy Customization Apps & 3D Printing to Kids."
37. Quoted in Steve Crowe, "Meet Cannybots: 3D Printable Robot Cars Blowing Up on Kickstarter," Robotics Trends, September 29, 2015. www.roboticstrends.com.
38. Seth Colander, "3DRudder VR Foot Controller Steering Towards March Launch," Tom's Hardware, January 15, 2016. www.tomshardware.com.
39. Lily Prasuethsut and Hugh Langley, "Hands On: PlayStation VR Review," TechRadar, September 15, 2015. www.techradar.com.
40. Quoted in Nicole Arce, "'Minecraft' Getting Virtual Reality Treatment, Will Come to the Oculus Rift and Gear VR in 2016," *Tech Times*, September 28, 2015. www.techtimes.com.
41. Michael Rundle, "'Dreams' Sculpts Games from Your Subconscious," *Wired*, October 28, 2015. www.wired.co.uk.

42. Virtual Reality Site, "Augmented Reality," 2015. www.vrs.org
.uk.
43. Quoted in Charles Q. Choi, "Cautious Optimism About Micro-soft's HoloLens," *IEEE Spectrum*, January 26, 2015. http://spectrum.ieee.org.
44. Quoted in Choi, "Cautious Optimism About Microsoft's Ho-loLens."

Chapter Five: Museums and Theme Parks

45. Craig Hanna, "Museum of the Future," Thinkwell, December 16, 2015. https://thinkwellgroup.com.
46. Quoted in Josef Hargrave and Radha Mistry, *Museums in the Digital Age*. London: ARUP, 2013, p. 5.
47. Jessica Gelt, "How Museums Are Adapting to 'Selfie Cul-ture,'" *Los Angeles Times*, October 23, 2015. www.latimes.com.
48. Quoted in Smithsonian Newsdesk, "Smithsonian Brings His-toric Specimens to Life in Free "Skin and Bones" Mobile App," January 13, 2015. http://newsdesk.si.edu.
49. Quoted in John Gaudiosi, "Virtual Reality, Augmented Reality Theme Park Being Built in China," *Fortune*, June 18, 2015. http://fortune.com.
50. Quoted in Suzy Strutner, "Six Flags Offers a Bone-Chilling Virtual Ride on New 'Joker' Coaster," *Huffington Post*, September 4, 2015. www.huffingtonpost.com.
51. Quote in Carly Ledbetter, "Cedar Point's New Roller Coaster Has a Terrifying 214-Foot Drop," *Huffington Post*, September 9, 2015. www.huffingtonpost.com.
52. Dave Smith, "Inside the Void: An Exclusive Look at the Future of Virtual Reality," *Tech Insider*, September 15, 2015. www.techinsider.io.
53. Rachel Metz, "Inside the First VR Theme Park," *MIT Technology Review*, December 15, 2015. www.technologyreview.com.
54. Quoted in Sonia Weiser, "5 Educated Predictions for the Future of Amusement Parks," *Mental_Floss*, May 26, 2015. http://mentalfloss.com.

For Further Research

Books

Matthew Anniss, *The Impact of Technology in Music*. Hampshire, UK: Raintree, 2015.

Betsy Cassriel, *Robot Builders!* Broomall, PA: Mason Crest, 2015.

Katie Cunningham, *Next-Gen Coders*. Sebastopol, CA: O'Reilly, 2016.

Brook Drumm et al., *3D Printing Projects: Toys, Bots, Tools, and Vehicles to Print Yourself*. San Francisco: Maker Media, 2015.

Nick Willoughby, *Digital Filmmaking for Kids*. Hoboken, NJ: For Dummies, 2015.

Websites

BBC Future (www.bbc.com/future). The British Broadcasting Corporation runs this site with in-depth coverage of cutting edge science, health, and technology. The site covers everything from the environment and the Internet to transportation systems of tomorrow.

Cardboard (www.google.com/get/cardboard/get-cardboard). Consumers who wish to turn their smartphones into 3D-viewing devices can visit this website with instruction, schematics, and a list of parts needed to build the Google Cardboard virtual reality mount.

Gizmag (www.gizmag.com). Gizmag covers virtual reality gear, high-tech TVs, movies, cameras, and new and emerging technologies, inventions, innovations, and science. The site provides reliable reviews, news, photos, blogs, and videos for tech lovers.

Tech Insider (www.techinsider.io). This website covers all things tech with links dedicated to science, innovation, culture, and trending topics. Videos and articles cover virtual reality, movie and TV tech, and the latest trends in music and digital art.

TechRadar (www.techradar.com). Visitors to this website can see the latest news about phones, laptops, wearable tech, car tech, and gaming equipment. Readers can learn the science and history behind the latest gadgets and view photos and videos.

Using the Sun to Make Music, YouTube. (www.youtube.com /watch?v=kcqiLvHiACQ). This ten-minute documentary about Robert Alexander shows how the composer takes data generated by the sun and turns it into music through the sonification process.

Virtual Reality Site (www.vrs.org.uk). This site explores concepts, news, and resources central to VR, including the use of the technology for gaming, education, military, and health care. There are links to articles on history, apps, guides, and gear, and a section on augmented reality.

Index

Picture Credits

Cover: © Colin Anderson/Blend Images/Corbis

4: Depositphotos

5: Depositphotos

7: Depositphotos

11: Depositphotos

12: Detlev van Ravenswaay/Science Photo Library

18: © Photoshot

22: Depositphotos

24: Depositphotos

28: © Colin Anderson/Blend Images/Corbis

34: Photofest Images

37: Photofest Images

40: © Artic-Images/Corbis

46: Depositphotos

48: Bizu Tesfaye/Sipa USA/Newscom

51: Martyn Landi/Zuma Press/Newscom

59: © Thomas Hartwell/Corbis

62: Hal Beral/Newscom

66: Depositphotos